DK WORKBOOKS

K **Spelling**

Author Linda Ruggieri

DK | Penguin Random House

Editors Jolyon Goddard,
Nishtha Kapil, Margaret Parrish
Assistant Editor Shahwar Kibria
Art Editors Dheeraj Arora, Jyotsna Julka
Managing Editor Soma B. Chowdhury
Managing Art Editors Richard Czapnik,
Ahlawat Gunjan
Producer, Pre-Production Francesca Wardell
Producer Christine Ni
DTP Designer Anita Yadav

First American Edition, 2015
Published in the United States by DK Publishing
345 Hudson Street, New York, New York 10014

A catalog record for this book
is available from the Library of Congress.
ISBN: 978-1-4654-2915-5

DK books are available at special discounts when purchased
in bulk for sales promotions, premiums, fund-raising, or
educational use. For details, contact:
DK Publishing Special Markets,
345 Hudson Street, New York, New York 10014
SpecialSales@dk.com

Printed and bound in China

All images © Dorling Kindersley Limited
For further information see: www.dkimages.com

A WORLD OF IDEAS:
SEE ALL THERE IS TO KNOW
www.dk.com

Contents

This chart lists all the topics in the book.
Once you have completed each page,
stick a star in the correct box below.

FACTS

We spell words with letters. A set of these letters is called the alphabet. Each letter has a different shape and sound.

Read the letters of the alphabet aloud or sing them.

A a

apple

B b

ball

C c

cat

D d

door

E e

egg

F f

feet

G g

gate

H h

hen

I i

ice

J j

jar

K k

kite

L l

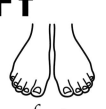

lamp

M m

mop

N n

nest

O o

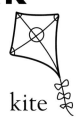

octopus

P p

pencil

The alphabet has 26 letters. Each letter has an uppercase and a lowercase form.

Q q

queen

R r

rabbit

S s

sun

T t

turtle

U u

umbrella

V v

violin

W w

watch

X x

x-ray

Y y

yak

Z z

zipper

Write the letter that begins the name of each picture below.

__pple

__en

__est

FACTS

Activities using the alphabet help children identify, read, and write uppercase and lowercase letters.

Trace the uppercase and lowercase letters of the alphabet wherever they are missing.

Matching the uppercase and lowercase letters of the alphabet helps children with reading and writing.

Draw a line from each sock on the top clothesline to the sock with the matching lowercase letter on the bottom clothesline.

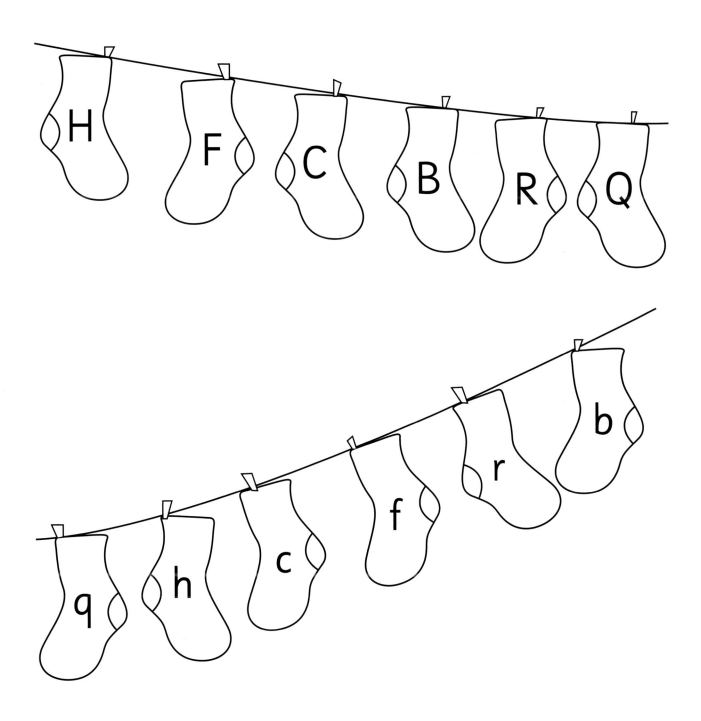

Vowels and Consonants

FACTS

Words are spelled with letters. Some letters are consonants and some are vowels. The letters **a, e, i, o,** and **u** are vowels. The letter **y** is sometimes a vowel and sometimes a consonant. The other letters of the alphabet are consonants.

Read each picture's name aloud. Circle the vowel you hear in the middle of each word.

sun   bed   hen   log

cat   pin   pup   wig

Look at each picture and write the consonant that begins the name of each picture.

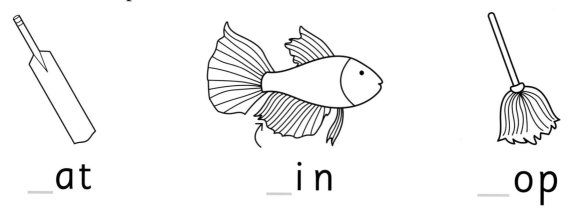

_at   _in   _op

Each letter has a different sound. For example, the letters **b-a-t** spell "bat." The letters **b-u-g** spell "bug."

Look at each picture and say its name aloud. Then write the letters of its name in the boxes in the correct order.

bat

bug

dig

dog

fin

fan

sun

sit

cup

cat

mat

mop

FACTS

The letter **b** begins the word "book." The letter **c** begins the word "cat." The letter **d** begins the word "duck." The letter **f** begins the word "fun."

Trace the uppercase and lowercase letters in each row. Circle the picture in each row whose name begins with the same letter.

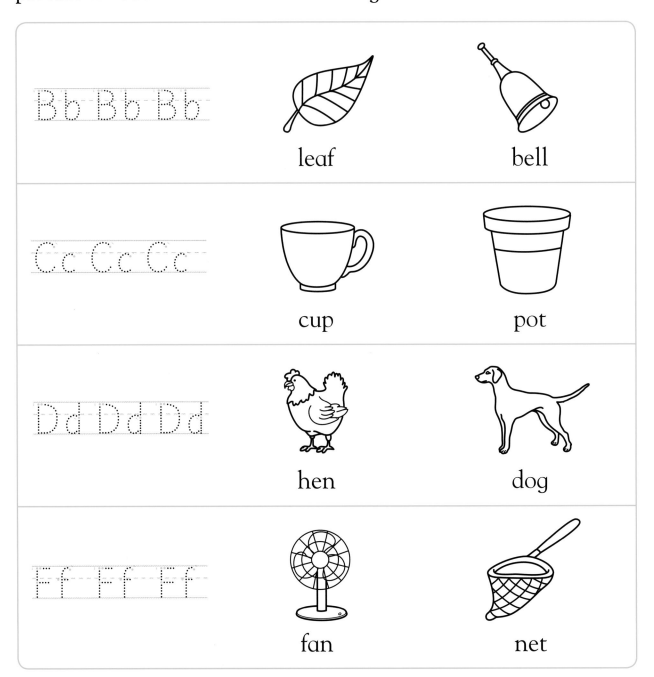

Bb Bb Bb

leaf   bell

Cc Cc Cc

cup   pot

Dd Dd Dd

hen   dog

Ff Ff Ff

fan   net

The letter **g** begins the word "gift." The letter **h** begins the word "hut." The letter **j** begins the word "jump." The letter **k** begins the word "kite."

Trace the uppercase and lowercase letters in each row. Circle the picture in each row whose name begins with the same letter.

Gg Gg Gg   gate   boat

Hh Hh Hh   house   mouse

Jj Jj Jj   jam   duck

Kk Kk Kk   kite   bed

FACTS

The letter **l** begins the word "lamp." The letter **m** begins the word "mop." The letter **n** begins the word "net." The letter **p** begins the word "pan."

Trace the uppercase and lowercase letters at the beginning of each row. Circle the two words in each row that begin with the same letter.

Ll Ll Ll

leaf   log   candle

Mm Mm Mm

mug   boot   moon

Nn Nn Nn

nurse   nest   swing

Pp Pp Pp

puppy   bat   pencil

The letter **q** begins the word "quilt." The letter **r** begins the word "rabbit." The letter **s** begins the word "sock." The letter **t** begins the word "top."

Trace the uppercase and lowercase letters at the beginning of each row. Circle the two words in each row that begin with the same letter.

queen   quilt   cat

robot   door   rug

soap   bus   sun

tiger   boat   tent

FACTS

The letter **v** begins the word "van." The letter **w** begins the word "window." The letter **x** begins the word "x-ray." The letter **y** begins the word "yard." The letter **z** begins the word "zebra."

Trace the uppercase and lowercase letters at the beginning of each row. Circle the word or words in each row that begin with the same letter.

Vv Vv Vv   van   pin   vase

Ww Ww Ww   worm   fan   window

Xx Xx Xx   x-ray   book   chick

Yy Yy Yy   yak   yogurt   shoe

Zz Zz Zz   zebra   zipper   sun

Words have different sounds based on the order of the letters they contain. If the beginning, middle, or final letters of a word change, a new word with a different sound is made.

Read each pair of words below. Then underline the letters that are different in each pair.

box fox

pen pan

coat boat

rug run

hen ten

nail pail

FACTS

Each letter in a word has a different sound. Identifying the initial sound of a word helps you to say it.

Read each picture's name on the left. Using a letter from the box, complete the rhyming picture's name on the right.

| h | p | f |

can   _an

bat   _at

cup   _up

fin   _in

pen   _en

Recognizing simple consonant-vowel-consonant words builds knowledge of words, their sounds, and spellings.

Read each picture's name on the left. Using a vowel from the box, complete the picture's name on the right.

o	a	u

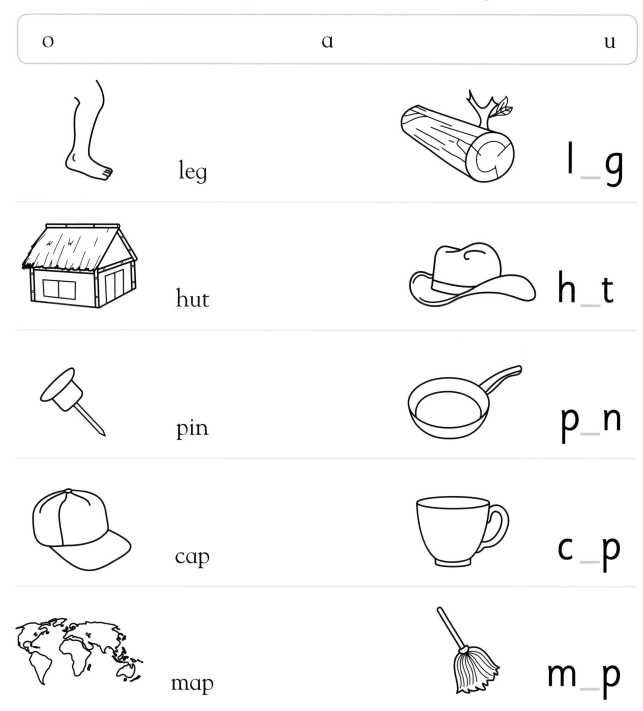

leg   l _ g

hut   h _ t

pin   p _ n

cap   c _ p

map   m _ p

FACTS

The ending sounds of words can be short or extended. Some letters produce short, or stop, sounds, such as the **t** in "bat." Other words end with extended, or continuous, letter sounds. For example, the letter **r** can be extended in "far."

Look at the first picture in each row. Read its name aloud. Look at the other two pictures in the row. Find the picture's name that ends in the same sound as the first picture's name. Circle that picture and its name.

man   web   run

 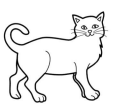 

bat   cat   dog

star   bell   car

Words can be broken up into letters and the sounds of the letters.

Read the words aloud and write each letter in a separate box.

bug

pin

hen

net

web

fan

bus

pup

FACTS

The long sound of the vowel **a** says its name. You hear the long "a" sound in the word "snake."

Read each picture's name aloud. Circle the names of the six pictures that have the long "a" sound. Make an **X** on the names of the two pictures that have the short "a" sound, as heard in "cat."

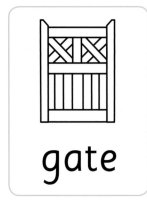 gate

 whale

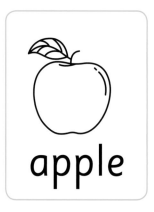 face

 apple

 cake

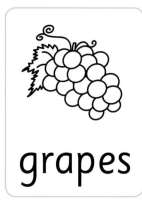 grapes

 bat

 train

Read the sentence below. Circle the two words that have the long "a" sound.

Owen and I like to play in the rain.

The long sound of the vowel **e** says its name. You hear the long "e" sound in the word "cheese."

Read each picture's name aloud. Circle the names of the six pictures that have the long "e" sound. Make an **X** on the names of the two pictures that have the short "e" sound, as heard in "pen."

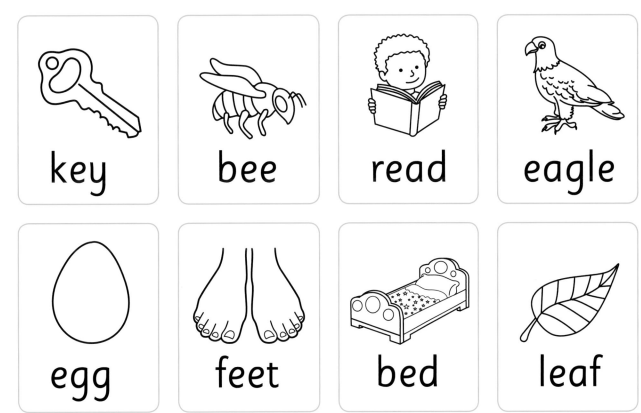

key

bee

read

eagle

egg

feet

bed

leaf

Fill in the letter **e** to complete the long "e" names of the bunny's body parts.

t __ __ th   f __ __ t

FACTS

The long sound of the vowel **i** says its name. You hear the long "i" sound in the word "lion."

Read each picture's name aloud. Circle the names of the six pictures that have the long "i" sound. Make an **X** on the names of the two pictures that have the short "i" sound, as heard in "tin."

ice

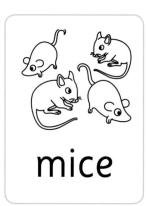

mice

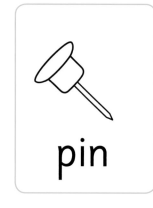

pin

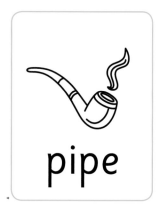

pipe

fish

kite

dice

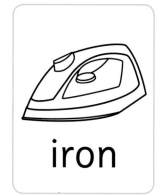

iron

Read the sentence below. Circle the two words that have the long "i" sound.

The tiger is a big cat that has stripes.

The long sound of the vowel **o** says its name. You hear the long "o" sound in the word "boat."

Read each picture's name aloud. Circle the names of the six pictures that have the long "o" sound. Make an **X** on the names of the two pictures that have the short "o" sound, as heard in "pot."

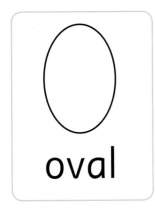

oval

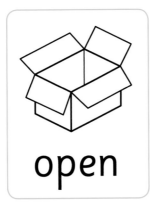

open

goat

mop

yogurt

log

toast

soap

Read the sentence below. Circle the two words that have the long "o" sound.

Jenny likes to eat yogurt and toast.

The long sound of the vowel **u** says its name. You hear the long "u" sound in the word "cube."

Read the words on the balloons aloud. Color the five balloons that have words with the long "u" sound. Make an **X** on the two balloons that have words with the short "u" sound, as heard in "fun."

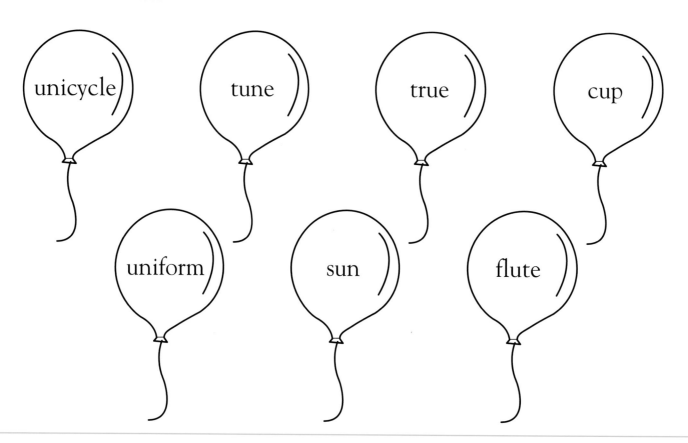

unicycle   tune   true   cup

uniform   sun   flute

Read the sentence below. Circle the three words that have the long "u" sound.

Brandon is using a tube of glue.

FACTS

The letter **y** can be tricky. Sometimes, it makes the long "e" vowel sound, as in the word "funny." Sometimes, it makes the long "i" vowel sound, as in the word "sky."

Circle the letter **y** in each word below. Read the word aloud. Listen to the "e" sound **y** makes in each word.

 puppy

 bunny

 lady

 happy

 candy

 baby

Write the letter **y** to complete each word below. Read the word aloud. Listen to the "i" sound **y** makes in each word.

 sk_

 fl_

 cr_

 fr_

 b_e

 sp_

FACTS

The word "apple" begins with the short sound of the vowel **a**. Some other words with the short "a" sound are "ax," "bag," and "rat."

Circle the names of the four pictures that have the short "a" sound. Make an **X** on the names of the two pictures that have the long "a" sound.

cat   hand   cake

bag   whale   can

For each word below, fill in the letter **a** to complete the word.

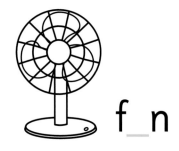
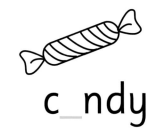

h_t   f_n   c_ndy

The word "egg" begins with the short sound of the vowel **e**. You also hear the short "**e**" sound in the words "elbow," "desk," and "hen."

Read each picture's name in the word wheel aloud. Color each section of the wheel in which the picture's name has the short "e" sound.

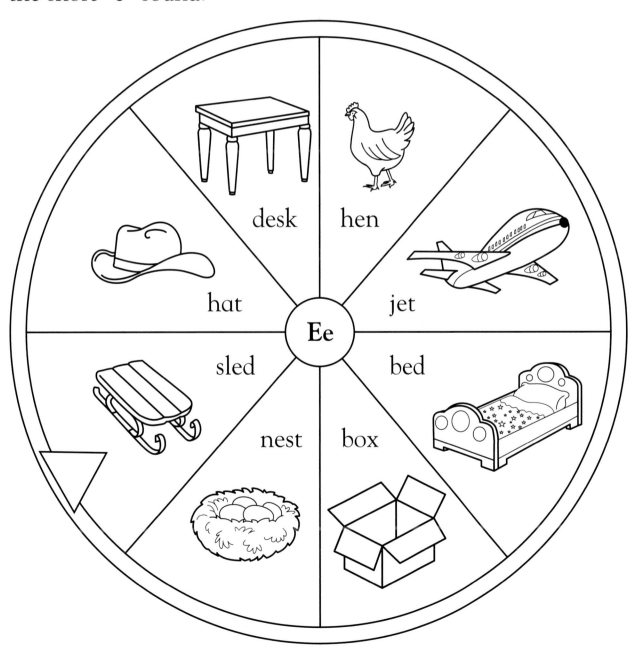

FACTS

The word "pin" has the short sound of the vowel **i**. You also hear the short "i" sound in the words "pig," "fin," and "fish."

Read each picture's name in the word wheel aloud.
If the word has the short "i" sound, underline the letter **i**.
Make an **X** on the words that have the long "i" sound.

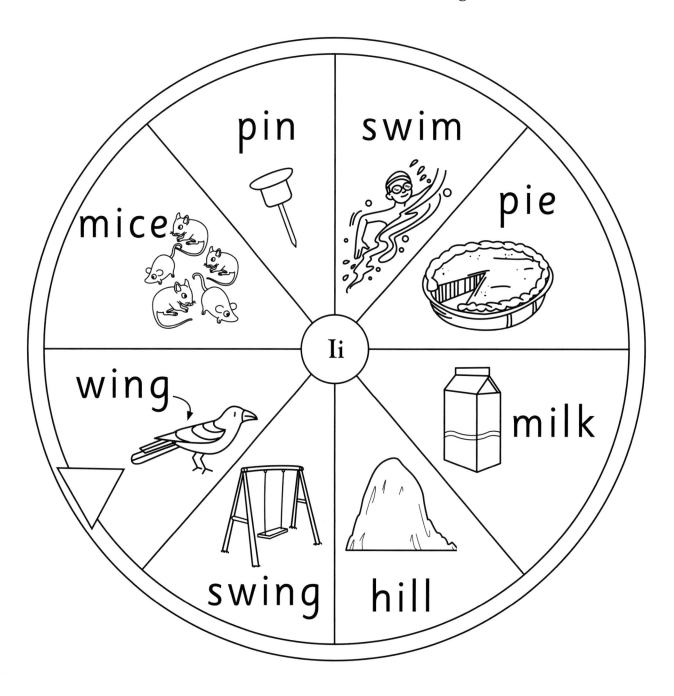

FACTS

The word "dog" has the short sound of the vowel **o**. You also hear the short "o" sound in the words "top" and "mop."

Read each picture's name aloud. Circle the six names that have the short "o" sound. Make an **X** on the two names that have the long "o" sound.

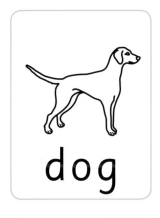 dog

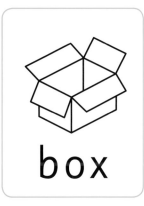 box

 soap

 mop

 log

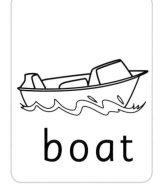 boat

 fox

 sock

Read the sentence below. Circle the three words that have the short "o" sound.

The dog jumped over a log to run after the frog.

The word "umbrella" has the short sound of the vowel **u**. You also hear the short "u" sound in the words "drum," "pup," and "sun."

Read each picture's name aloud. Circle the six names that have the short "u" sound. Make an **X** on the two names that have the long "u" sound.

drum

cup

unicorn

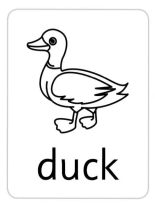

duck

sun

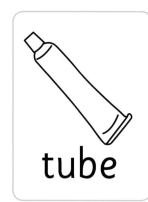

tube

jump

under

Read the sentence below. Circle the three words that have the short "u" sound.

The bug is snug in the rug.

The individual letter sounds in simple words can be changed to make new words.

Read each picture's name on the left. Fill in the letter to complete the picture's name on the right.

box

_ ox

jet

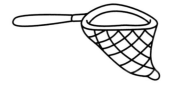
_ et

bug

_ ug

hen

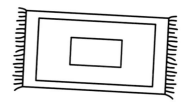
_ en

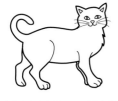
cat

_ at

fan

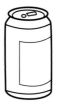
_ an

FACTS

To identify spoken words, let your child listen to the beginning sounds of the words.

Look at the picture of each animal. Say the letter on the animal aloud. Then draw a line to match each animal to its name.

monkey

lion

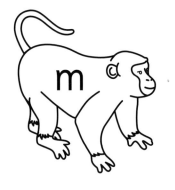

fish

zebra

FACTS

Rhyming words have the same ending sound. For example, "cap" and "nap" end with the same letter sound.

Read the pictures' names in each box aloud. Circle "yes" if the words rhyme and "no" if the words do not rhyme.

cat   mat

yes   **no**

pan   can

yes   **no**

sun   box

yes   **no**

mop   top

yes   **no**

hat   bat

yes   **no**

jet   net

yes   **no**

pig   wig

yes   **no**

dig   pin

yes   **no**

Every word has one or more syllables, or beats. For example, the word "boat" has one syllable, the word "butter" has two syllables, and the word "dinosaur" has three syllables.

Read each animal's name aloud. As you say the word, count the number of its syllables. Circle the correct number.

lion

| 1 | 2 | 3 |

fish

| 1 | 2 | 3 |

horse

| 1 | 2 | 3 |

elephant

| 1 | 2 | 3 |

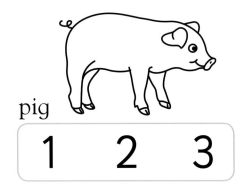

pig

| 1 | 2 | 3 |

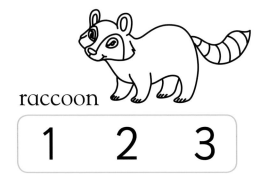

raccoon

| 1 | 2 | 3 |

Every syllable has one vowel sound. For example, the word "tomato" has three vowel sounds and three syllables.

Read each sentence aloud. Circle the number of syllables in each underlined word.

My snack today is a banana.

1   2   3

Do you have any crayons?

1   2   3

Turn off the radio.

1   2   3

Let's bake a cake.

1   2   3

Let's sit at the table.

1   2   3

I see an orange butterfly.

1   2   3

FACTS

Sight words, or high-frequency words, are words commonly used in speaking and writing. The spelling of some of these words does not follow the usual letter-sound pattern.

Practice reading and using the sight words listed below.

all	four	on	too
am	get	please	under
are	good	ran	was
at	have	say	what
be	he	she	who
but	into	so	will
came	like	that	with
did	no	there	yes
do	now	they	you
eat	of	this	your

Learning to spell and use sight words improves fluency in reading.

Read each sentence below. Circle the correct sight word to complete the sentence.

I know the days of has the week.

Do you your have a red crayon?

Does she her have a brother?

That girl be is my friend.

Kate went to am the zoo.

A cat is in so the tree.

FACTS

Words are made with letters that are placed in order from left to right.

Find the words from the word box in the rectangles below.
Each rectangle has three words hidden in it.
Circle the words and read them aloud.

bat	cat	milk	rat	horse
drum	doll	kiwi	pear	

Food Words

p e a r g o j k i w i q v m i l k

Toy Words

d o l l r j h i b a t x d r u m x

Animal Words

c a t j z p r a t g u i h o r s e

Print, or written text, is made up of letters and words that are read from left to right.

Read the words in each sentence aloud. Circle the word at the end of each line.

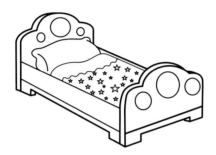

I see a bed.

I see a tree.

I see a horse.

I see a jar.

I see a kite.

Words in a sentence are read from left to right.
At the end of a line, you return to the left side
of the next line to continue reading.

Draw a line from the word in the box to the same word
on the right.

 James has a ball .   ball

The dog is on the chair .   chair

 Sara has a flower .   flower

The bird is in a nest .   nest

 Clarissa has a book .   book

Words are combined to form sentences. The words in a sentence are separated by a single space between each word.

The sentences below tell a story. Count the words in each sentence. Circle the number of words each sentence contains.

I have a bear.

1 2 3 4 5 6 7

It is a brown bear.

1 2 3 4 5 6 7

It is not a big bear.

1 2 3 4 5 6 7

The little bear sits in a chair.

1 2 3 4 5 6 7

My little bear is a teddy bear.

1 2 3 4 5 6 7

Each sentence ends with a punctuation mark, such as a period (.).

Look at each sentence below. The spaces between words are missing. Draw a line between the letters where each space should be. Add a period at the end of each sentence.

Icanjump

Ilikeswings

Mycatisasleep

Icanflyakite

A sentence is a group of words that expresses a complete thought. Sentences can be long or short.

Read each sentence aloud. Count the words in each sentence and circle the correct number.

I like ice cream.

1   2   3   4   5   6

I like vanilla ice cream.

1   2   3   4   5   6

I like vanilla ice-cream cones.

1   2   3   4   5   6

I like rainbow sprinkles, too.

1   2   3   4   5   6

Complete the sentence below.

My favorite ice-cream flavor is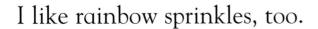

Count the words above. Write the number.

FACTS

Sentences that end with rhyming words are called rhyming sentences. Some poems have rhyming sentences.

Read each sentence aloud. Look at each picture and pick the correct word to complete the rhyme.

The dog has a toy mouse.

The dog is in a ....

house   hut

The boy has a pet duck.

The duck sat in the ....

wagon   truck

The pig lives in a pen.

The pig is named ....

Bob   Ben

Kate saw a ladybug.

The ladybug was on a ....

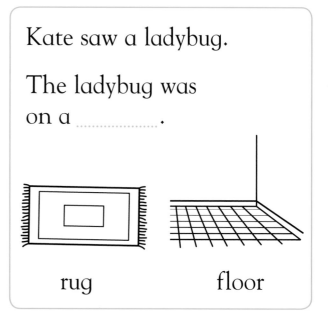

rug   floor

You read words from left to right, top to bottom, and then page by page.

The pictures in the boxes below tell a story. Follow the numbers to read the story and answer the questions.

1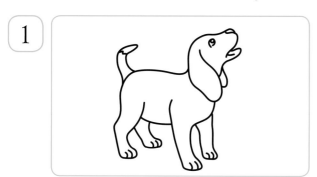

The puppy barks.

2

The puppy is given food.

3

The puppy eats her food.

4

Finally, the puppy sleeps.

In which picture does the puppy bark?

In which picture does the puppy eat?

In which picture does the puppy sleep?

In which picture is the puppy given food?

FACTS

Knowing the sounds that letters make helps children recognize words and builds reading skills.

Read the story aloud. Circle the correct word to answer each question.

A Puppy Named Pooky

Joey has a little puppy.
She is a funny puppy.
The puppy is named Pooky.
One day, Pooky went to hide.
Where are you, Pooky?
Pooky was under the table.

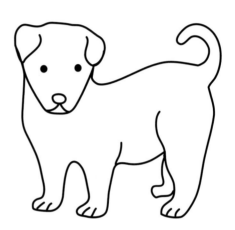

What is the story about?

a cat   a puppy

Is the puppy big or little?

big   little

What is the name of the puppy?

Joey   Pooky

Where was Pooky hiding?

under the table   under the bed

Children should be able to read with purpose and understanding. Regular reading reinforces fluency so that children read accurately, quickly, and with expression.

Read all about the life of a frog in the four boxes.
Pick the correct word to complete each sentence below.

The Life of a Frog

1. "Ribbit!" That may be a frog calling. Let's visit the pond. Frogs live on land and in water.

2. Many frogs eat insects. They use their long tongues to catch them.

3. Frogs have long, strong back legs. They are good jumpers and swimmers.

4. Frogs lay eggs. The eggs hatch into tadpoles. The tadpoles grow up to be frogs.

Frogs live on land and in ....   water   caves

Many frogs eat ....   insects   fish

Frogs have long back ....   tails   legs

Frogs are good ....   jumpers   crawlers

Certificate

Congratulations to

....

for successfully
finishing this book.

GOOD JOB!

You're a star.

Date

....

Answer Section with Parents' Notes

This book is intended to introduce basic spelling skills to your child. By working through this book, your child will practice key Common Core State Standards (CCSS) for kindergarten spelling, which are vital to his or her understanding of letters, words, and sentences.

Contents

These activities are intended to be completed by a child with adult support. The topics covered are:

- letters of the alphabet;
- uppercase and lowercase letters;
- vowels and consonants;
- long and short vowel sounds;
- consonant sounds;
- understanding the sequence of letters to learn words;
- initial, middle, and final sounds in CVC (consonant-vowel-consonant) words;
- syllables;
- common sight words, such as "the," "of," "to," "you," "she," "my," "is," and "are";
- understanding print and learning to read sentences;
- reading kindergarten-level text with fluency, purpose, and understanding.

How to Help Your Child

As you work through the pages with your child, make sure he or she understands what each activity requires. Read the facts and instructions aloud. Encourage questions and reinforce observations that will build confidence and increase active participation in classes at school.

By working with your child, you will understand how he or she thinks and learns. This workbook is designed to help your child understand the concept of letters and words. When appropriate, use props such as pictures or flash cards to help your child visualize letters and words.

If an activity seems too challenging, encourage your child to try another page. Good luck, and remember to have fun!

5

Letters of the Alphabet

We spell words with letters. A set of these letters is called the alphabet. Each letter has a different shape and sound.

Read the letters of the alphabet aloud or sing them.

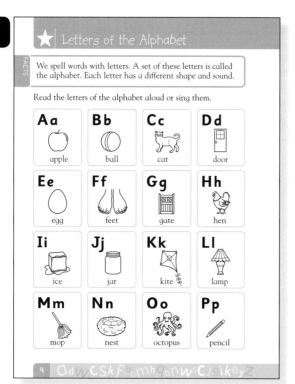

Letters of the Alphabet

The alphabet has 26 letters. Each letter has an uppercase and a lowercase form.

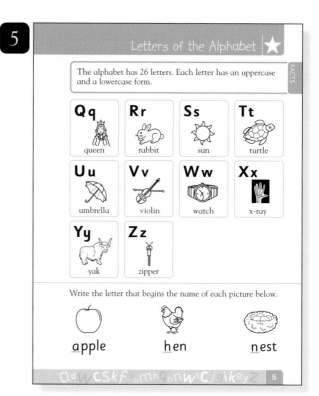

Write the letter that begins the name of each picture below.

apple   hen   nest

You can make a set of reusable cards from pages 4 and 5. Photocopy the pages, laminate them, and then cut out the individual letter cards. You may want to glue cord onto the letters before laminating them so that your child can touch and feel each letter.

Review each letter with your child and work together to come up with places where he or she has seen the letter—perhaps in a name, on a sign, or in his or her city, town, or street address.

Uppercase and Lowercase

Activities using the alphabet help children identify, read, and write uppercase and lowercase letters.

Trace the uppercase and lowercase letters of the alphabet wherever they are missing.

Matching Letters

Matching the uppercase and lowercase letters of the alphabet helps children with reading and writing.

Draw a line from each sock on the top clothesline to the sock with the matching lowercase letter on the bottom clothesline.

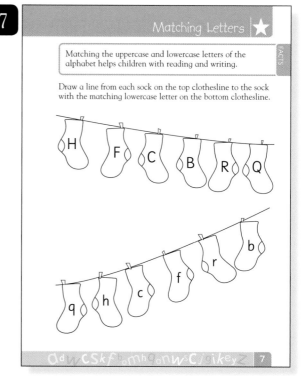

This activity gives your child practice in writing uppercase and lowercase letters and forming them correctly. Ask your child to say the name of each letter aloud as he or she traces it.

This activity will help your child have a better understanding of corresponding uppercase and lowercase letters. Use pages 4 and 5, or the cards you made, to review other corresponding uppercase and lowercase letters.

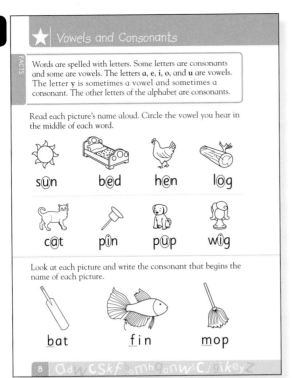

8

★ Vowels and Consonants

Words are spelled with letters. Some letters are consonants and some are vowels. The letters **a**, **e**, **i**, **o**, and **u** are vowels. The letter **y** is sometimes a vowel and sometimes a consonant. The other letters of the alphabet are consonants.

Read each picture's name aloud. Circle the vowel you hear in the middle of each word.

s**u**n   b**e**d   h**e**n   l**o**g

c**a**t   p**i**n   p**u**p   w**i**g

Look at each picture and write the consonant that begins the name of each picture.

bat   fin   mop

Teach your child to distinguish vowels from consonants. Let him or her sort letter blocks or cards into vowels and consonants while saying each letter. Say some simple words and ask your child to identify the middle vowel. For example, "What's the middle letter in the word 'hat'?"

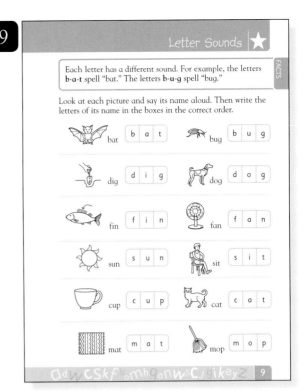

9

Letter Sounds ★

Each letter has a different sound. For example, the letters **b-a-t** spell "bat." The letters **b-u-g** spell "bug."

Look at each picture and say its name aloud. Then write the letters of its name in the boxes in the correct order.

bat | b a t   bug | b u g

dig | d i g   dog | d o g

fin | f i n   fan | f a n

sun | s u n   sit | s i t

cup | c u p   cat | c a t

mat | m a t   mop | m o p

Help your child connect sounds to printed text. This provides a way for your child to approach new words. Help him or her say the sound of each letter in the words above. Practice this often when you talk about new words.

10

★ Consonants b, c, d, and f

The letter **b** begins the word "book." The letter **c** begins the word "cat." The letter **d** begins the word "duck." The letter **f** begins the word "fun."

Trace the uppercase and lowercase letters in each row. Circle the picture in each row whose name begins with the same letter.

Bb Bb Bb	leaf	bell
Cc Cc Cc	cup	pot
Dd Dd Dd	hen	dog
Ff Ff Ff	fan	net

Find pictures of things that begin with **b**, **c**, **d**, and **f**. Label small boxes with the letters. Play a sorting game. Let your child say the name of each picture and then place it in the correct box.

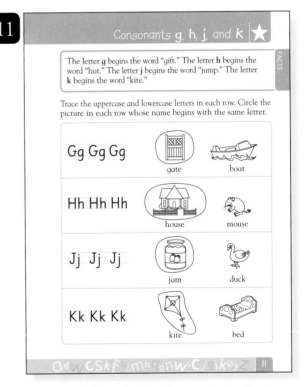

Consonants g, h, j, and k ★

The letter **g** begins the word "gift." The letter **h** begins the word "hut." The letter **j** begins the word "jump." The letter **k** begins the word "kite."

Trace the uppercase and lowercase letters in each row. Circle the picture in each row whose name begins with the same letter.

Gg Gg Gg	gate	boat
Hh Hh Hh	house	mouse
Jj Jj Jj	jam	duck
Kk Kk Kk	kite	bed

Ask your child to think of five words that begin with **g**, five words that begin with **h**, five that begin with **j**, and five that begin with **k**. Offer help if your child needs it. You could also add that **g** sometimes has a **j** sound, as in the word "gentle."

⭐ Consonants **l**, **m**, **n**, and **p**

FACTS
The letter **l** begins the word "lamp." The letter **m** begins the word "mop." The letter **n** begins the word "net." The letter **p** begins the word "pan."

Trace the uppercase and lowercase letters at the beginning of each row. Circle the two words in each row that begin with the same letter.

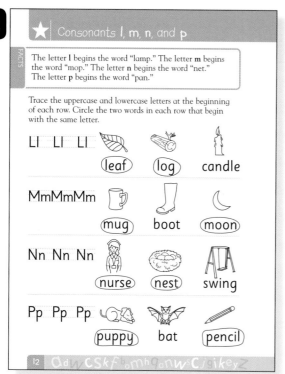

Ll Ll Ll   (leaf) (log) candle

MmMmMm   (mug) boot (moon)

Nn Nn Nn   (nurse) (nest) swing

Pp Pp Pp   (puppy) bat (pencil)

Play the sorting game again. Find pictures of things that begin with **l**, **m**, **n**, and **p**. Label small boxes with the letters. Let your child say the name of each picture and then place it in the correct box.

13

Consonants **q**, **r**, **s**, and **t** ⭐

FACTS
The letter **q** begins the word "quilt." The letter **r** begins the word "rabbit." The letter **s** begins the word "sock." The letter **t** begins the word "top."

Trace the uppercase and lowercase letters at the beginning of each row. Circle the two words in each row that begin with the same letter.

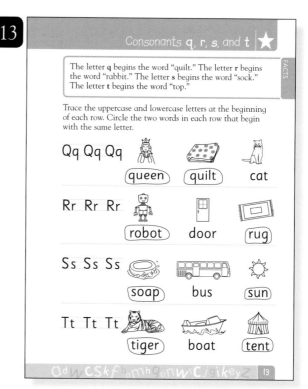

Qq Qq Qq   (queen) (quilt) cat

Rr Rr Rr   (robot) door (rug)

Ss Ss Ss   (soap) bus (sun)

Tt Tt Tt   (tiger) boat (tent)

Reinforce how to pronounce the letters **q**, **r**, **s**, and **t**. Say words beginning with these letters and let your child repeat each word aloud. Words could include "quarter," "round," "super," and "tongue."

14

⭐ Consonants **v**, **w**, **x**, **y**, and **z**

FACTS
The letter **v** begins the word "van." The letter **w** begins the word "window." The letter **x** begins the word "x-ray." The letter **y** begins the word "yard." The letter **z** begins the word "zebra."

Trace the uppercase and lowercase letters at the beginning of each row. Circle the word or words in each row that begin with the same letter.

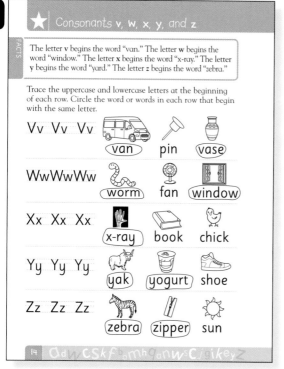

Vv Vv Vv   (van) pin (vase)

WwWwWw   (worm) fan (window)

Xx Xx Xx   (x-ray) book chick

Yy Yy Yy   (yak) (yogurt) shoe

Zz Zz Zz   (zebra) (zipper) sun

Ask your child to think of more words that begin with or contain these less commonly used consonants. Examples include "voice," "wand," "fox," "you," and "pizza." Don't forget to remind your child that the letter **y** is sometimes used as a vowel, too.

Letter Sounds ⭐

FACTS
Words have different sounds based on the order of the letters they contain. If the beginning, middle, or final letters of a word change, a new word with a different sound is made.

Read each pair of words below. Then underline the letters that are different in each pair.

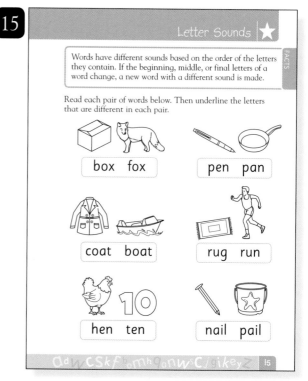

box fox   pen pan

coat boat   rug run

hen ten   nail pail

Practice sounding out the initial and other sounds of words. Make sure your child understands the terms beginning, or initial, middle, and ending sounds. Use the word "hen," for example, and exaggerate the sound of each letter.

★ Beginning Sounds

FACTS Each letter in a word has a different sound. Identifying the initial sound of a word helps you to say it.

Read each picture's name on the left. Using a letter from the box, complete the rhyming picture's name on the right.

h	p	f

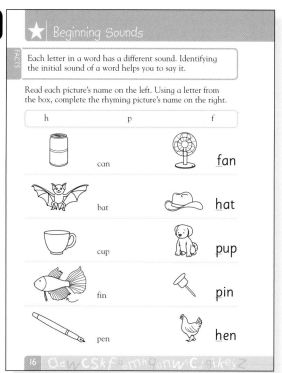

can   **f**an

bat   **h**at

cup   **p**up

fin   **p**in

pen   **h**en

Write rhyming words on index cards, using specific-colored markers for each group of words. For example, red for words ending in "-up," blue for words ending in "-at," and green for words ending in "-ad." Let your child identify the rhyme and sort the cards into groups.

Middle Vowel Sounds ★

FACTS Recognizing simple consonant-vowel-consonant words builds knowledge of words, their sounds, and spellings.

Read each picture's name on the left. Using a vowel from the box, complete the picture's name on the right.

o	a	u

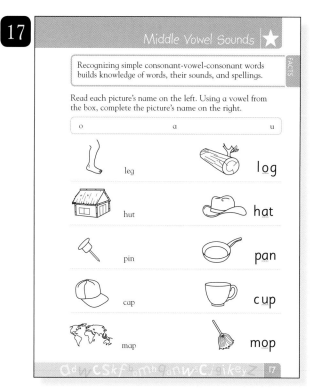

leg   l**o**g

hut   h**a**t

pin   p**a**n

cap   c**u**p

map   m**o**p

Reinforce sounds and letters. Use a dark marker to write the five vowels at the bottom of five small paper cups. After working on the page, review the 10 words and ask your child to identify the paper cup with the correct vowel for each word.

★ Final Sounds

FACTS The ending sounds of words can be short or extended. Some letters produce short, or stop, sounds, such as the **t** in "bat." Other words end with extended, or continuous, letter sounds. For example, the letter **r** can be extended in "far."

Look at the first picture in each row. Read its name aloud. Look at the other two pictures in the row. Find the picture's name that ends in the same sound as the first picture's name. Circle that picture and its name.

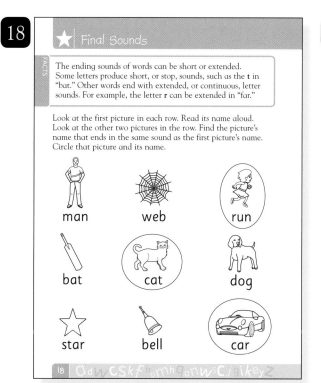

man   web   run

bat   cat   dog

star   bell   car

Read the words "sun" and "moon." Ask your child if they end with the same sound. Then say the words "door" and "book." Ask if they end with the same sound. Explore saying and writing words with the same ending sounds as "door." Examples are "floor," "car," and "your."

Different Letter Sounds ★

FACTS Words can be broken up into letters and the sounds of the letters.

Read the words aloud and write each letter in a separate box.

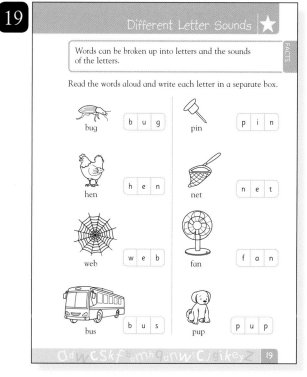

bug | b | u | g | pin | p | i | n |

hen | h | e | n | net | n | e | t |

web | w | e | b | fan | f | a | n |

bus | b | u | s | pup | p | u | p |

As an extension to this activity, find some more simple consonant-vowel-consonant words and practice breaking these words up into sounds with your child.

★ The Long "a" Sound

The long sound of the vowel **a** says its name. You hear the long "a" sound in the word "snake."

Read each picture's name aloud. Circle the names of the six pictures that have the long "a" sound. Make an **X** on the names of the two pictures that have the short "a" sound, as heard in "cat."

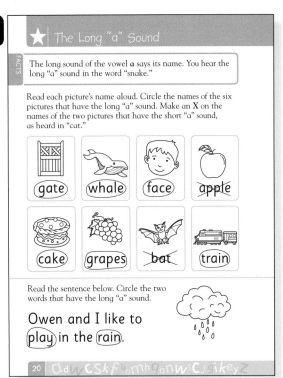

gate whale face apple
cake grapes bat train

Read the sentence below. Circle the two words that have the long "a" sound.

Owen and I like to (play) in the (rain).

Reinforce that long vowel sounds say the name of the vowel. Use a set of cards or magnetic letters and say each vowel. With your child, write a list of words with the long "a" sound.

The Long "e" Sound ★

The long sound of the vowel **e** says its name. You hear the long "e" sound in the word "cheese."

Read each picture's name aloud. Circle the names of the six pictures that have the long "e" sound. Make an **X** on the names of the two pictures that have the short "e" sound, as heard in "pen."

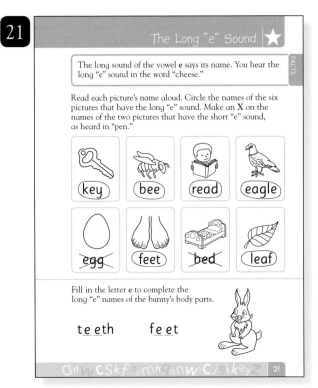

key bee read eagle
egg feet bed leaf

Fill in the letter **e** to complete the long "e" names of the bunny's body parts.

te e th   fe e t

Help your child distinguish the long vowel sound of the letter **e** from the short "e" sound. Find pictures of things with both sounds. Engage him or her in sorting the pictures into two containers, one labeled "short vowel" and the other "long vowel."

★ The Long "i" Sound

The long sound of the vowel **i** says its name. You hear the long "i" sound in the word "lion."

Read each picture's name aloud. Circle the names of the six pictures that have the long "i" sound. Make an **X** on the names of the two pictures that have the short "i" sound, as heard in "tin."

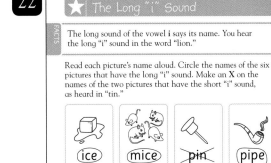

ice mice pin pipe
fish kite dice iron

Read the sentence below. Circle the two words that have the long "i" sound.

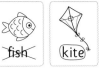

The (tiger) is a big cat that has (stripes).

Cut a large piece of construction paper into the shape of a kite and attach a tail with a piece of string. With your child, find and write the long "i" words on small cards. Tape the cards to the tail. Use these words to write a poem with your child.

The Long "o" Sound ★

The long sound of the vowel **o** says its name. You hear the long "o" sound in the word "boat."

Read each picture's name aloud. Circle the names of the six pictures that have the long "o" sound. Make an **X** on the names of the two pictures that have the short "o" sound, as heard in "pot."

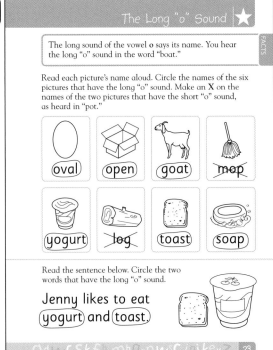

oval open goat mop
yogurt log toast soap

Read the sentence below. Circle the two words that have the long "o" sound.

Jenny likes to eat (yogurt) and (toast).

Draw an oval on a large sheet of paper. Write some long "o" and short "o" words on small cards. Guide your child to identify and then tape the cards with long "o" words onto the oval.

★ The Long "u" Sound

The long sound of the vowel **u** says its name. You hear the long "u" sound in the word "cube."

Read the words on the balloons aloud. Color the five balloons that have words with the long "u" sound. Make an **X** on the two balloons that have words with the short "u" sound, as heard in "fun."

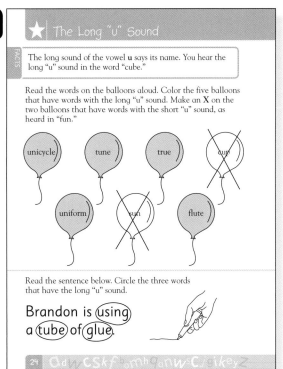

unicycle   tune   true   ~~cup~~

uniform   ~~sun~~   flute

Read the sentence below. Circle the three words that have the long "u" sound.

Brandon is (using) a (tube) of (glue).

Review the long "u" sound by writing a short rhyme with your child. For example, "Does the boy in blue have the glue?" or "The unicorn wore a uniform."

The Tricky Letter y ★

The letter **y** can be tricky. Sometimes, it makes the long "e" vowel sound, as in the word "funny." Sometimes, it makes the long "i" vowel sound, as in the word "sky."

Circle the letter **y** in each word below. Read the word aloud. Listen to the "e" sound **y** makes in each word.

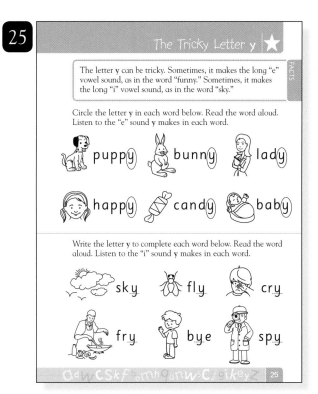

puppy   bunny   lady

happy   candy   baby

Write the letter **y** to complete each word below. Read the word aloud. Listen to the "i" sound **y** makes in each word.

sky   fly   cry

fry   bye   spy

Say words that end in the letter **y**, emphasizing the final sound, such as "carry," "silly," "sly," "spy," "lucky," "hungry," "why," and "dry." Ask your child to hold up a card showing the letter **e** or **i**, depending on the sound of **y** in each word.

★ The Short "a" Sound

The word "apple" begins with the short sound of the vowel **a**. Some other words with the short "a" sound are "ax," "bag," and "rat."

Circle the names of the four pictures that have the short "a" sound. Make an **X** on the names of the two pictures that have the long "a" sound.

cat   hand   ~~cake~~

bag   ~~whale~~   can

For each word below, fill in the letter **a** to complete the word.

hat   fan   candy

Give your child a card with the letter **a**. Then give him or her a card with a consonant and ask your child to place the consonant before the **a**. Ask him or her to think of words that begin with those two letters. Finally, ask whether each word has a long or short "a" sound.

The Short "e" Sound ★

The word "egg" begins with the short sound of the vowel **e**. You also hear the short "e" sound in the words "elbow," "desk," and "hen."

Read each picture's name in the word wheel aloud. Color each section of the wheel in which the picture's name has the short "e" sound.

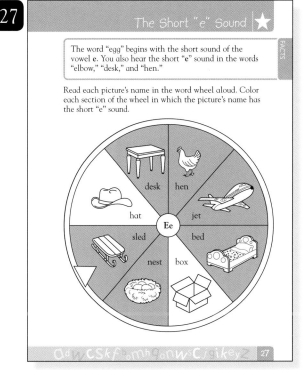

desk   hen   jet   bed   box   nest   sled   hat

Ee

Reinforce the sounds of the letter **e**. List words with both long and short "e" sounds. Read them randomly. Let your child show an index card labeled "long" or "short" based on the letter sound he or she hears in each word. Examples include "pet," "bean," "met," "meet," "red," and "bead."

★ The Short "i" Sound

FACTS

The word "pin" has the short sound of the vowel **i**. You also hear the short "i" sound in the words "pig," "fin," and "fish."

Read each picture's name in the word wheel aloud.
If the word has the short "i" sound, underline the letter **i**.
Make an **X** on the words that have the long "i" sound.

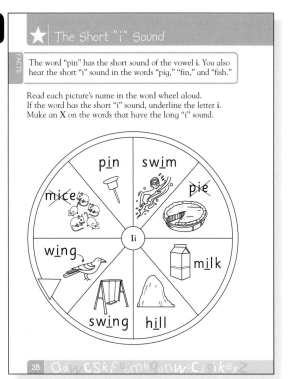

p<u>i</u>n

swim

pie

mice

Ii

m<u>i</u>lk

w<u>i</u>ng

sw<u>i</u>ng

h<u>i</u>ll

Help your child see words in context. Write sentences with short "i" words. Read them aloud, emphasizing the short "i" words. Then ask which words have the short "i" sound. An example of a sentence could be "The *little pig* had a curly tail."

The Short "o" Sound ★

FACTS

The word "dog" has the short sound of the vowel **o**. You also hear the short "o" sound in the words "top" and "mop."

Read each picture's name aloud. Circle the six names that have the short "o" sound. Make an **X** on the two names that have the long "o" sound.

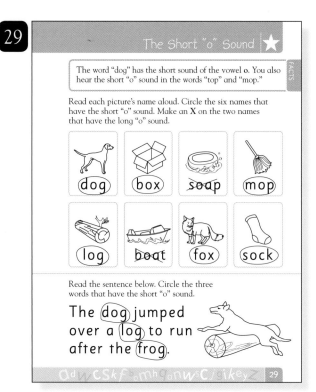

dog   box   soap   mop

log   boat   fox   sock

Read the sentence below. Circle the three words that have the short "o" sound.

The dog jumped over a log to run after the frog.

Record your voice reading words with the short "o" sound. Let your child read some words and record his or her voice. Listen to the recording as you view a list of words that includes those recorded. Help your child identify and highlight the words he or she hears.

★ The Short "u" Sound

FACTS

The word "umbrella" has the short sound of the vowel **u**. You also hear the short "u" sound in the words "drum," "pup," and "sun."

Read each picture's name aloud. Circle the six names that have the short "u" sound. Make an **X** on the two names that have the long "u" sound.

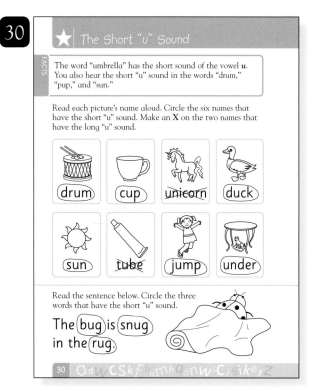

drum   cup   unicorn   duck

sun   tube   jump   under

Read the sentence below. Circle the three words that have the short "u" sound.

The bug is snug in the rug.

Read pairs of words, such as "run fun," "pan can," and "bump jump." Some words should have the short sound of the letter **u**, and the others should not. Let your child show a thumbs-up for the pairs with the short "u" sound and a thumbs-down for the others.

Letters and Words ★

FACTS

The individual letter sounds in simple words can be changed to make new words.

Read each picture's name on the left. Fill in the letter to complete the picture's name on the right.

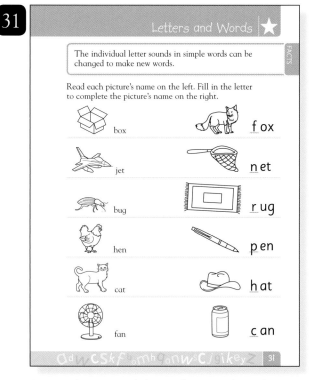

box   f ox

jet   n et

bug   r ug

hen   p en

cat   h at

fan   c an

Practice letter sounds by emphasizing those that your child may find challenging to hear and identify. Examples are "n" and "m," "b" and "p," and "d" and "t." Have your child show a letter card when he or she hears a particular sound.

★ Beginning Sounds

FACTS To identify spoken words, let your child listen to the beginning sounds of the words.

Look at the picture of each animal. Say the letter on the animal aloud. Then draw a line to match each animal to its name.

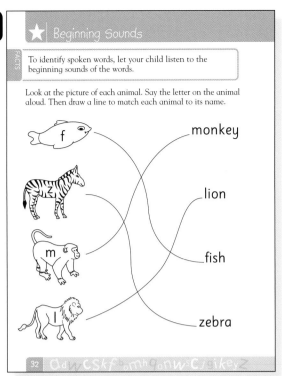

monkey

lion

fish

zebra

After your child works on this page, encourage him or her to think of more animal names. Ask your child to tell you the beginning letter of each name.

Rhyming Words ★

FACTS Rhyming words have the same ending sound. For example, "cap" and "nap" end with the same letter sound.

Read the pictures' names in each box aloud. Circle "yes" if the words rhyme and "no" if the words do not rhyme.

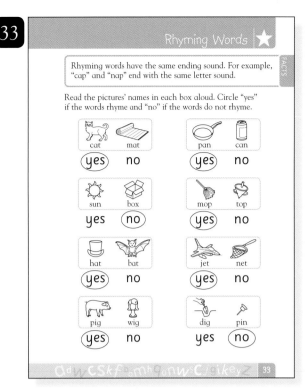

Read nursery rhymes aloud with your child. Emphasize the rhyming words. Let your child see the words and guide him or her to point to the words that rhyme.

★ Syllables

FACTS Every word has one or more syllables, or beats. For example, the word "boat" has one syllable, the word "butter" has two syllables, and the word "dinosaur" has three syllables.

Read each animal's name aloud. As you say the word, count the number of its syllables. Circle the correct number.

lion   1 ② 3
fish   ① 2 3
horse   ① 2 3
elephant 1 2 ③
pig   ① 2 3
raccoon 1 ② 3

While you are working through this page, bang on a toy drum or a metal pot to emphasize the number of syllables in each word. After that, encourage your child to say names of family members and friends and count the number of syllables in each name.

More Syllables ★

FACTS Every syllable has one vowel sound. For example, the word "tomato" has three vowel sounds and three syllables.

Read each sentence aloud. Circle the number of syllables in each underlined word.

My snack today is a banana.
1   2   ③

Do you have any crayons?
1   ②   3

Turn off the radio.
1   2   ③

Let's bake a cake.
①   2   3

Let's sit at the table.
1   ②   3

I see an orange butterfly.
1   2   ③

Guide your child to create a few sentences and help him or her write them down. In each sentence, examine the words and in each word, the syllables. Encourage him or her to count the syllables. Dinosaur names, such as "stegosaurus," can be particularly exciting examples.

★ Sight Words

FACTS

Sight words, or high-frequency words, are words commonly used in speaking and writing. The spelling of some of these words does not follow the usual letter-sound pattern.

Practice reading and using the sight words listed below.

all	four	on	too
am	get	please	under
are	good	ran	was
at	have	say	what
be	he	she	who
but	into	so	will
came	like	that	with
did	no	there	yes
do	now	they	you
eat	of	this	your

Write these words on cards. With your child, practice using them to create sentences. The next time you are reading a story with your child, encourage him or her to identify sight words in the text.

FACTS

Learning to spell and use sight words improves fluency in reading.

Read each sentence below. Circle the correct sight word to complete the sentence.

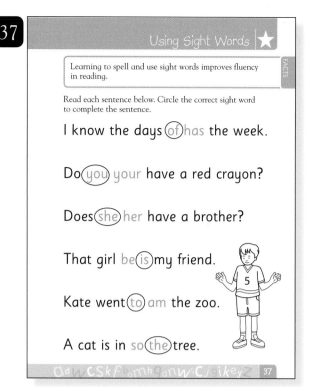

I know the days (of) has the week.

Do (you) your have a red crayon?

Does (she) her have a brother?

That girl be (is) my friend.

Kate went (to) am the zoo.

A cat is in so (the) tree.

Your child learns sight words, or high-frequency words, by repeatedly seeing and using them. Write sentences with the sight words missing. Let your child choose the word that makes the most sense.

★ Letters Make Words

FACTS

Words are made with letters that are placed in order from left to right.

Find the words from the word box in the rectangles below. Each rectangle has three words hidden in it. Circle the words and read them aloud.

bat	cat	milk	rat	horse
drum	doll	kiwi	pear	

Food Words

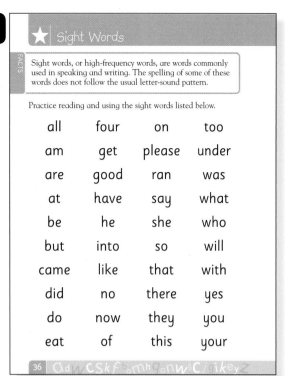

p e a r g o j k i w i q v m i l k

Toy Words

d o l l r j h i b a t x d r u m x

Animal Words

c a t j z p r a t g u i h o r s e

This activity will help your child distinguish words from random groups of letters. By seeing groups of concept words, he or she will see that words convey ideas and meanings. Introduce your child to simple word searches that contain three-letter words.

FACTS

Print, or written text, is made up of letters and words that are read from left to right.

Read the words in each sentence aloud. Circle the word at the end of each line.

I see a (bed).　　I see a (tree).

I see a (horse).

I see a (jar).　　I see a (kite).

If necessary, help your child follow the pattern of reading word by word. Place a small card under each word as you read from left to right to reinforce the reading process.

★ Reading from Left to Right

FACTS

Words in a sentence are read from left to right. At the end of a line, you return to the left side of the next line to continue reading.

Draw a line from the word in the box to the same word on the right.

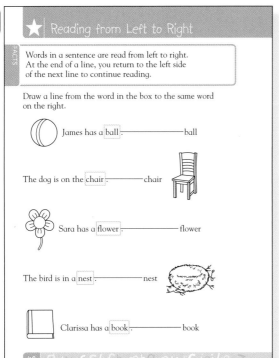

James has a ball ———— ball

The dog is on the chair ———— chair

Sara has a flower ———— flower

The bird is in a nest ———— nest

Clarissa has a book ———— book

While working through this page, reinforce the fact that each sentence conveys an idea or a thought. After reading, you could test your child on the spelling of some of the words on this page, such as "book," "nest," and "chair."

Reading and Counting Words ★

FACTS

Words are combined to form sentences. The words in a sentence are separated by a single space between each word.

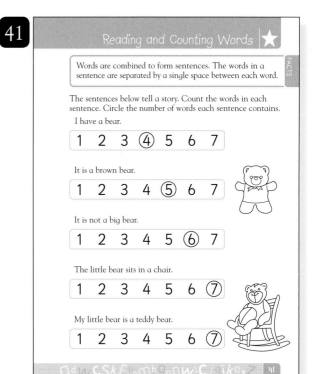

The sentences below tell a story. Count the words in each sentence. Circle the number of words each sentence contains.

I have a bear.

1　2　3　④　5　6　7

It is a brown bear.

1　2　3　4　⑤　6　7

It is not a big bear.

1　2　3　4　5　⑥　7

The little bear sits in a chair.

1　2　3　4　5　6　⑦

My little bear is a teddy bear.

1　2　3　4　5　6　⑦

Help your child gain confidence as a reader as he or she counts the words in a sentence successfully. Point out the use of uppercase letters to begin sentences and punctuation, such as periods, to end sentences.

★ Words Make Sentences

FACTS

Each sentence ends with a punctuation mark, such as a period (.).

Look at each sentence below. The spaces between words are missing. Draw a line between the letters where each space should be. Add a period at the end of each sentence.

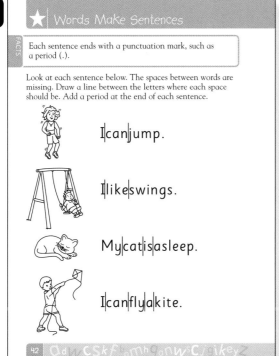

I|can|jump.

I|like|swings.

My|cat|is|asleep.

I|can|fly|a|kite.

Ask your child to look around him or her to think of some small sentences. Help your child to write them, and then draw attention to each word and its meaning. Encourage your child to use finger spaces between each word when writing.

Words Make Sentences ★

FACTS

A sentence is a group of words that expresses a complete thought. Sentences can be long or short.

Read each sentence aloud. Count the words in each sentence and circle the correct number.

I like ice cream.

1　2　3　④　5　6

I like vanilla ice cream.

1　2　3　4　⑤　6

I like vanilla ice-cream cones.

1　2　3　4　5　⑥

I like rainbow sprinkles, too.

1　2　3　4　⑤　6

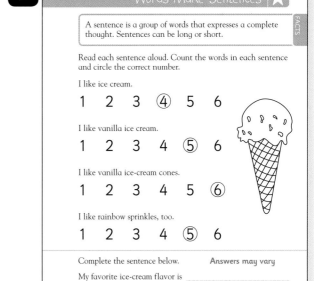

Complete the sentence below.　**Answers may vary**

My favorite ice-cream flavor is _____

Count the words above. Write the number. ☐

After completing this page, ask questions and guide your child to write simple sentences about one of his or her favorite things. Count the words in each sentence to show your child how he or she is forming ideas with words.

★ Rhyming Sentences

Sentences that end with rhyming words are called rhyming sentences. Some poems have rhyming sentences.

Read each sentence aloud. Look at each picture and pick the correct word to complete the rhyme.

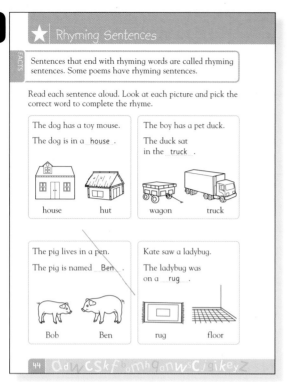

The dog has a toy mouse.
The dog is in a __house__ .

house   hut

The boy has a pet duck.
The duck sat in the __truck__ .

wagon   truck

The pig lives in a pen.
The pig is named __Ben__ .

Bob   Ben

Kate saw a ladybug.
The ladybug was on a __rug__ .

rug   floor

Your child will gain confidence as a reader as he or she reads each rhyme. Follow up this activity by reading simple poems from a book or from a website. Leave out some of the rhyming words and let your child fill them in.

Reading a Story ★

You read words from left to right, top to bottom, and then page by page.

The pictures in the boxes below tell a story. Follow the numbers to read the story and answer the questions.

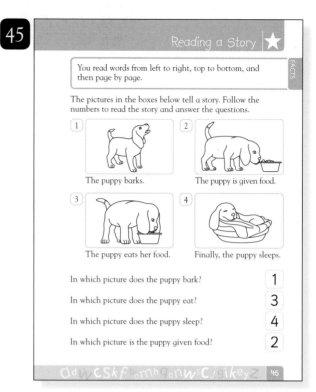

1. The puppy barks.
2. The puppy is given food.
3. The puppy eats her food.
4. Finally, the puppy sleeps.

In which picture does the puppy bark?   **1**
In which picture does the puppy eat?   **3**
In which picture does the puppy sleep?   **4**
In which picture is the puppy given food?   **2**

To check comprehension of the picture story on this page, ask questions such as "Why does the puppy bark?" Point out the numbers on each picture and reinforce that there is a sequence of events in the story.

★ Reading a Story

Knowing the sounds that letters make helps children recognize words and builds reading skills.

Read the story aloud. Circle the correct word to answer each question.

A Puppy Named Pooky

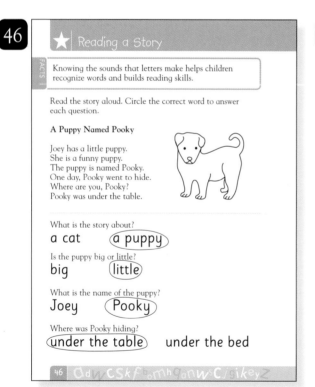

Joey has a little puppy.
She is a funny puppy.
The puppy is named Pooky.
One day, Pooky went to hide.
Where are you, Pooky?
Pooky was under the table.

What is the story about?
a cat   (a puppy)

Is the puppy big or little?
big   (little)

What is the name of the puppy?
Joey   (Pooky)

Where was Pooky hiding?
(under the table)   under the bed

Reading words and listening to their sounds carefully is a step toward comprehending text. As your child listens to a story, he or she begins to see that words have meaning. Check his or her understanding of text. Read the text slowly, then repeat it. Review it before asking questions.

Reading to Understand ★

Children should be able to read with purpose and understanding. Regular reading reinforces fluency so that children read accurately, quickly, and with expression.

Read all about the life of a frog in the four boxes. Pick the correct word to complete each sentence below.

The Life of a Frog

1. "Ribbit!" That may be a frog calling. Let's visit the pond. Frogs live on land and in water.

2. Many frogs eat insects. They use their long tongues to catch them.

3. Frogs have long, strong back legs. They are good jumpers and swimmers.

4. Frogs lay eggs. The eggs hatch into tadpoles. The tadpoles grow up to be frogs.

Frogs live on land and in __water__ . | water   caves

Many frogs eat __insects__ . | insects   fish

Frogs have long back __legs__ . | tails   legs

Frogs are good __jumpers__ . | jumpers   crawlers

Let your child listen to the real-life information on this page one or two times before he or she answers the questions. If your child does not recall the information, show him or her how to look back at the text to find answers.